Different Voices
Shared Lives

Dedicated to the memory of Perry Lee

Writing on the Wall
Toxteth Library
Windsor Street, Liverpool
L8 1XF

Published by Writing on the Wall, 2022

Design and Layout by Jenny Dalton
Cover Design by Po.Ke Marketing

978-1-910580-85-1

0151 703 0020
info@writingonthewall.org.uk
www.writingonthewall.org.uk

Content Warning:
This book contains potentially sensitive content including: racism, strong language, racial slurs and violence.

Table of Contents

Foreword

As a conurbation established around a port city, the Liverpool City Region's entire identity is built on the meeting and melding of people, personalities, and creativity. In the more than eight hundred years since Liverpool was established, our culture has been enriched by this continued evolution.

From our humble beginnings as a small fishing village to our status as a centre of global trade, the region has a long and storied past. But there are some regretful chapters to our story that we cannot shy away from.

Like many port cities around the world, our region played a shameful and prominent role in the transatlantic slave trade – a legacy that we are still coming to terms with today.

While it can be uncomfortable to face up to the entirety of our past, it is imperative that we are transparent about every aspect of our history, even those that we are not proud of. History gives us an opportunity to learn, to reflect, and to remember the lessons and mistakes of the generations before us – and ensure that they are never repeated.

Today, our region's diversity is one of our greatest strengths – it enhances our culture, enriches our lives, and makes our area one of the best places in the country to live and work. While we've come so far on our journey, it's clear that there's still a lot of work to be done to tackle racial inequality.

Different Voices, Shared Lives is a commemoration of the different circumstances that have brought each of the authors here, the trails and tribulations they have faced, and the lives they are building for themselves in our region.

It is a remarkable and deeply moving anthology of short stories, poems, and personal experiences. But above all, it is an incredible distillation of our shared history, our hopes for a better future, and the creative genius that makes our region great.

The authors might come from different backgrounds. They have taken different routes to get here, facing different challenges along the way. But what unites them all is a sense of belonging. Each of them is now interwoven in the fabric of the Liverpool City Region. All have a role to play in writing the next chapter in the illustrious history of our region.

As the region's Mayor, it is my enormous privilege to be able to support projects like this; to give a platform to ordinary members of our region to tell their stories, and to shine a light on underrepresented communities who too often struggle to have their voice heard.

Working together, it is my hope that we can build a fairer, more equal Liverpool City Region, where no one is left behind.

Metro Mayor Steve Rotheram

Introduction

"Until the lions have their own historians, the history of the hunt will always glorify the hunter."
- *Chinua Achebe*

At Writing on the Wall, we are committed to expanding our understanding of history and the development of our communities. Through such Creative Heritage work as the George Garrett Archive, the Great War to Race Riots and the L8 Archive Projects, we have worked alongside community members to uncover our hidden histories, providing platforms for those whose stories have been excluded from popular narratives. Liverpool City Region has a wonderfully diverse population, home to the oldest black and Chinese communities in Europe, yet outside of the city little has been documented about these communities. Even in Liverpool where black and other racial minority communities are largest, there is still much work to be done.

In *Different Voices Shared Lives*, 'the lions' share their own stories, in their own words. In doing so they expand our understanding of both the neighbourhoods that make up our City Region and the myriad of global connections that we have. *Different Voices Shared Lives* gives new insights into the region's culture and heritage and brings to the foreground new and powerful voices.

This incredible collection of writing by members of black, Asian, and other racial minority communities is the culmination of an extensive creative writing programme. This was delivered in partnership with the City Region's six library services, in which professional writers supported the development of new writing talent. It offered creative platforms and pathways for people from diverse communities across the Region to express themselves, explore, discuss, and tell of their historical and contemporary experiences of living and working in the region. Writing on the Wall would like to thank all the writers who worked on the project; Amina Atiq, Natalie Denny, Kiara Mohammed, Janaya Pickett and Blue Saint for the work that they have helped to inspire in this ground-breaking initiative.

Reaching people whose communities have been marginalised is not an easy task and we would not have met many of the writers in this collection without the Halton, St Helens, Sefton, Wirral, Knowsley and Liverpool Library Services and their partners. They provide vital services and community support, our partners included: Our Warm Welcome, Share Knowsley, Wirral Change, and the Venus Centre. Writing on the Wall would like to thank all these partners for the wonderful work that they do and also our thanks go to Rania Al Khllo who helped the writers overcome language barriers.

The final word must go to the writers in this collection.

The writing is brave, original and of such high quality. The stories represent a wealth of experience and at times are painful to read but these is joy, laughter, and hope; hope for new beginnings, where we learn from our individual and collective past. This collection is a powerful tool for promoting empathy, respect and cohesion and is a beautiful celebration of the diversity of the Liverpool City Region.

Madeline Heneghan
Co-Director, Writing on the Wall

Horizon
Sayed Jafar Rastin

There is a short distance between innocent and oppression

I learnt this from watching a young child, chasing ants, to kill them

Home

Coming Home
Angelita Woosnam

It was only when we got to the arrivals hall and saw the queue for immigration where we had to show our passports and say why we were here that I had the thought, what if they don't let us in? It hadn't occurred to me that this could even be a possibility. I should have thought about it really. After all, I had been deported from Australia many years ago but that's another story.

Arriving in Jamaica for the first time was exciting but I also felt very nervous. Waiting in line to go through immigration I wished – I suddenly wished – I had a different passport and could join the other queue – the one for people coming home.

I was travelling with an ex-partner, the father of my children, and that was a bit neve wracking too. Although we had three children between us and had lived together thirty years ago, the furthest we had travelled together had been Ireland once a year and we had both changed so much in those intervening years.

When we got to the desk to show our passports the lady asked us for an address where we were staying and I realised that I had forgotten that we needed to have this ready. I panicked and began to feel sick because I didn't have it written down. I couldn't phone my sister as I had no credit on my phone which created more panic in me.

Luckily, they had encountered this before and asked for the phone number and called her themselves. She of course gave them the address and we could go through immigration. Those few minutes whilst we waited for the official to say she had the address were scary and I did feel very shaky.

My shakiness and annoyance only lasted a little while though and was then replaced with excitement as we went through to collect our cases and leave the airport building. I felt a huge sense of relief wash over me.

My sister and her husband were waiting outside for us. He had driven round the block a couple of times because we had taken so long to come out of the airport. The big hug that she gave me helped to release some of the tension that I was feeling and I began to relax.

This was only the third time we had met – once in London forty years before and then two years before this in New York. She is my half-sister and a couple of years older than me, but we never use the half bit.

We drove into Kingston which reminded me of being in India in the late 1990s which was another adventure. It was easy to see remnants of the colonial history of Jamaica in the old buildings that we passed.

We collected food on the way and began to climb up above Kensington to their house on the hill. This felt a bit surreal as they lived in a very well-off part of the town in a large house behind an electric gate and I noticed that all the windows had shutters of bars on them. We didn't go in the front door but entered through the garage and then the kitchen before we saw the beautiful interior of their house.

My initial reaction was that it looked like a small hotel and when I saw my room I felt like I was in a hotel – it was huge. This was the beginning of a ten day adventure in the land where my parents were born and the one they left in 1954 to come to England.

Journeys For Work
Jeanette Francis

I had left the Caribbean Island of Grenada and after an eight-hour flight touched down at Heathrow airport the following morning. It was September 1978, cold with a grey sky. Years ago, the four seasons were distinct, so different to what we are experiencing now. It was a shock to my system to say the least. Formalities done at the passport checks, I made a journey to my sister-in-law's house in Tottenham Court Road, North London. Later that night, I boarded the midnight coach to Scotland where I resided for a year. I worked in a restaurant in Glasgow's west end called 'The Ubiquitous Chip.' Some of the football players were regular customers. The owners were Ian and Ronnie. One of the waitresses came to my flat and informed me that I had got the job.

The year I spent in Scotland was the best. I never experienced any form of racism or discrimination (consciously or unconsciously) even though I was the only black staff member and the only female assistant in the kitchen. The two chefs were Danny, who made us laugh as he was a character, and Jim. We worked well together. It was hard work starting at 6pm and finished around 3 or 4am. The pay was not great, but the cost of living was very cheap. The shopping bill was around £6. The first coat I bought was from a charity shop and I got my moneys worth, which was very little.

The weather was atrocious, and I slipped and fell several times on the snow because my footwear was unsuitable. Reflecting, I think, because of the hatred some of the Scottish people directed towards the English and also the hatred based on the sectarian divide between Celtic and Rangers football fans, maybe there was no more hatred left to direct at black people (that is my opinion). There were not many minorities, as far as I can remember, and almost all would have been employed at the hospitals including my husband. I was eventually to work at the hospital myself, after our move to Liverpool.

My working day began with the alarm going off at 5am. Normally I left at 6am and returned around 10pm after doing a twelve-hour shift. It felt like my head barely hit the pillow when the familiar noise of the alarm clock sounded again the next day. *Another five minutes* I would tell myself, but I knew that I couldn't indulge otherwise I would miss the vital connecting bus that took me to my destination. The cold, dark mornings were challenging yet it had to be done. I have a strong work ethic, but personally, I do not believe in the familiar saying that black people must work twice as hard.

My neighbours must have heard my footsteps as I made my way down to the bus stop. I enjoyed the light mornings with different birds and other animals contributing to the rich mixture of noises. The cat darting quickly underneath one of the cars parked at the side of the road. I thought, what is the reason cats behave in that manner? Dogs do not behave that way. There is a quietness, almost stillness, to early mornings as fewer vehicles are on the road. Most important I could see all around me that reassurance was welcoming.

On occasions I would come across one or two people wandering around aimlessly and my thoughts would wander back to the warm bed I just left. Do they not have a bed to go to? The corner shop would be opening at 6am and soon the regulars would be on their way to make purchases – noticeably newspapers. I arrived at the bus stop and there was a man, late thirties, or early forties I presumed. His face appeared pale with several noticeable lines, which conveyed to me that he was a drug abuser. A dog in need of some care sat beside him.

'Hiya girl,' was his opening line. I looked at him and before I could answer he said, '...I forgot you can't speak English.'

The next time I saw him he was walking towards me, again he repeated, 'hiya girl.'

My reply was 'I'm the woman you said cannot speak English.'

His reply conveyed how ignorant and racist he was as he said to the dog, 'Are you Chinese?'

I cannot understand what people like him are trying to achieve. Is it about making himself feel worthwhile, because he perceives himself above the black person in the hierarchal structure with privilege and power, therefore sees me as being inferior to him?

Not many passengers traveled that early in the morning, just a few regulars. Sometimes I took the opportunity to finish my sleep and hope I did not pass my stop to get off, as it could happen. Luckily, I was fully awake to get off where I should. I then waited for the second bus would take me to my destination, an NHS Trust in Lancashire. This ride was special, and I looked forward to it. The bus route took in the lovely countryside, quiet, peaceful, and idyllic. A sleepy little village with one shop doubling up as the post office.

One night, after leaving my workplace, I travelled on the run around bus to the train station then boarded the train to Liverpool Central Station. From central, I walked down to Sir Thomas Street where I normally catch the bus home. I noticed a few people waiting at different stops. It was well after 10pm. From the corner of my eyes, not far from where I was standing, I noticed two women were having a conversation. One of them was speaking loudly and anyone a few yards from her would have heard what she was disclosing.

Suddenly she turned to me and said, 'You all come over here and take our child benefit.'

This angry woman decided to blame me for not receiving child benefit because her children were now in care. This occurred in the eighties when I was younger and was not prepared to tolerate "any crap" from ignorant people in need of education. Someone who did not know their history, or worse, geography. My initial thought was she does not know me, and I was not prepared to put up with it. The woman wanted to have a physical fight with me. This happened during the eighties when the perception was that black people were to be more subservient.

I have never thought of myself as being afraid of standing up to anyone regardless of who they were. I give respect to people unconditionally, but those who try to be racist whether consciously or unconsciously, overtly, or subtle would quickly realise that I do not give in easily. I had more to lose than this woman, my job, and my reputation. I decided to deescalate the situation by telling her that I have just completed a twelve-hour shift looking after people like her and it worked.

Not being able to argue, she replied, 'Don't give me that.' Reflecting on racism, when I first came to Liverpool, I can recall two occasions when lads drove past and shouted the N word. Another involved a woman and dogs. The police were involved, and she was forced to write a letter of apology to me. My philosophy is trying not to generalise too much. When situations arise, deal with the individual or individuals in the now. Awareness has informed me that there are substantive factors that contribute to human behaviours. I have worked in environments both in the private and public sector and have not encountered much racism. I believe because, firstly, of the way I carry myself. I try not to give people the ammunition to make my life a living hell, especially in the workplace. Secondly, I make sure that I am valuable regarding work. As I said earlier, I do not believe that I must work twice as hard as my colleagues, when our wages and salaries are the same and they get promoted before I am.

The present situation is, in my opinion, a prime opportunity for increased racism and black people in particular must become more vigilant. I used to say to my Scottish friends, no one would know they are Scottish until they began speaking. I do not have to speak to determine that I am black.

Greenlight
Nargs Al Barzinji

I would like to tell you a part of my story.

When I came to the UK, it was a difficult life for me without my family. I did not know the language that well. I was depressed, sad, and anxious because of the life I had before. When I went to bed to sleep at night, all the memories of that life I had before woke me up and I would start crying without any reason.

One day I decided to change my life, I started watching motivational videos on YouTube to become a positive person and have positive thoughts towards everyone around me. One day a friend of mine recommended a book to read. The book she gave me has given me hope and a positive personality. I tried to open social media to learn English and I joined some groups on Facebook to communicate with other people from different countries so I could improve my language skills. At the same time, at my house, there were two friends and they were talking in English so I started to talk with them every single day. I remember it was one day that I wrote a quote on a piece of paper.

I said, 'God give me energy to help people as much as I can.'

Two months later, I started working with an organisation called 'Abetter.' This was a big step for me because from that day my life has changed. After all, it helped me to be strong. I was euphoric about a life of freedom. In this job, I was meeting new people, faced other people's problems, and helped a lot of them because I could understand them. I also started volunteering with British Red Cross and became an interpreter.

In the end, I want to say I love this country and I love the people here because they have helped me a lot.

DMP
Dawn Paisley Mills

My name is Dawn Paisley Mills, and I am from Chapeltown in Leeds. I have six sisters and seven brothers.

I first came to Liverpool in 1988 when my sister Diane (who had already run off to Liverpool) and her boyfriend were visiting Leeds and drove me over to Liverpool to enjoy the Liverpool 8 Carnival. I was hooked from that day and was fascinated by all the unusual shops and how cheap Liverpool was. I bought a pair of black boots from Wade Smith in the Cavern Quarter and some clothes in a shop called DoDos, which has now closed. Every month when I got paid, I would catch a £5 return coach to Liverpool station and spend all my money in DoDos then walk to my sister's house on Upper Parliament Street, have dinner and chill with her for the day before catching my coach back to Leeds.

In 1999, I finally decided to leave Leeds to catch a flight to America, to start a new life. While I was waiting for the day of my flight, I was staying with my sister on Upper Parliament Street. One day her doorbell rang, and she sent me downstairs to see who it was, and a white guy was standing outside her door holding my three-year-old nephew. I said to myself, *he's nice and he will make a good father.* He had black hair and gorgeous blue eyes and long eyelashes. I took my nephew from him and carried him upstairs to my sister.

I said to her, 'a white man brought your son home.'

She replied, 'Oh that's Sean. He goes to our church.'

So, I decided to go to church to get him and I used to sneak out of her house late at night to go see him when he invited me to come to his house. When the church found out that we were secretly seeing each other, they removed him from his position as church Deacon and accused him of sexual misconduct. My sister set about a witch hunt, so we both ran off, eloped to Scotland to meet his Scottish family. I decided not to go to America and we got married and had seven children.

I loved writing and drawing pictures when I was a child. I found it quite easy to rhyme words and I used to steal exercise books from the school store cupboard and cut them in half and make story books with pictures to match the stories. I liked reading nonsense poems and was influenced by famous poets such as Halaire Belloc of *Matilda who told lies and was burned to death,* Walter De La Mere, John Drinkwater, Lewis Carroll's *The Walrus and the Carpenter* and Dr Seuss' *The Cat in the Hat* fame who has the same writing style as myself, and likes to play with words repetitively, I am influenced by him.

My Home
Senait

Mezmur, the Church,
I pray in the morning.

Home gym; a good sport!
I learn English every day from life,
Twice a week in a class.

Doro Wot in the afternoon.
Injera at night.

I stroll through Kirkby,
My Home.

5th Generation

Janaya Pickett

We moved to the North end when I was four, after my parent's divorce. We lived off Country Road and less than a five-minute walk from Everton's football ground. This was the mid-late 1980's and my Mum would tell us to stay close to the house on match days. Occasionally I'd steer too far out of the Close and witness what looked, to my child mind, like an invasion of ghouls and zombies. Local white men stumbling out of local pubs in various states of consciousness.

A couple of times one grumbled at me 'nigger,' another 'black bastard.' One time one spat on the floor when we clocked eyes. Apart from one other group of siblings, we were the only black kids at our primary school. We were all (both sets of siblings totalling six) mixed race kids. In our case, Dad was black, Mum was white and in theirs the opposite was the case. But in 1980's Walton we were the blackest kids around. Apart from the occasional incident of outright racism, there was just the general knowledge that we were different and didn't fit in.

That changed when we moved to Liverpool 8 in the early 90's. My primary school class there looked like a poster campaign for United Colours of Benetton and I found it heavenly. I had black friends, a shared culture. But among them I was jokingly reminded of my 'white side,' not being able to braid my hair, having a white Mum (even though most of their Nan's were white), reading, listening to 'white music' and other things considered 'not black.' I learned about colourism when the friend I thought the most beautiful in the group was teased by other black boys for being 'too dark.' My skin and hair took on a desirability that I hadn't experienced before. It was confusing to a ten-year-old.

The contradictions in my old life and new were vast but largely anticipated, what surprised me were the contradictions in how others perceived me physically, just either side of town.

I had no knowledge of my black heritage; my Dad barely stayed in touch, he rolled around the UK like a stone. His immediate family had left Liverpool, like many of the black community in the 1970's, for London and I'd seen them a handful of times.

It wasn't until my mid-twenties, with the aid of ancestry.com, that I discovered my Dad's Mum didn't 'come off the banana boat,' post Windrush, as was the trope that I'd believed about the black presence in Liverpool. She was actually born here in 1942. I'd grown up feeling that although I was born in Liverpool, this is not where I'm really from, but in retrospect see I was a child believing the very narrow and incorrect tale offered by the institutions that governed her life. Finding out that my black Grandmother (her name was Eva) was born here emphasised a feeling I'd always had that was denied me as a black person in this city: Liverpool is home.

As the years passed, I found out much more about my black heritage. My Grandmother's Mother (Irene) was also a British born black women born in 1912. Her Mother (also Eva), my 2z Great Grandmother, was also a black woman, born in Bristol in 1885. She had 5 daughters and all of them by the 1920's were living at 1 Berkeley Street, Liverpool 8. She married a man named Howard Freeman whose occupation on their daughter Brenda's birth certificate is 'showman.' Irene was a 'music hall dancer' when she married. Her son, Jimmy Hinds, was a popular local singer during the 1950's and 1960's. I also discovered that there are Freeman's still living in Liverpool and connected with an auntie, who I'd known previously as a local legend and film producer, but not that we were related.

As technology advanced so did my research and through ancestry DNA, I connected with a distant relative living in Hawaii; a descendant of Benjamin Irons, the brother of my 3x Great-Grandfather (and Eva the first's father) Edward Irons. Edward came to Britain from South Carolina and married Sarah Ann James in 1883. I was sent a picture of his brother Benjamin: a smart looking dark black man with beautiful features, a moustache, a pocket watch. I wonder if Edward looked like him?

I also learned that Picture Post photographer Bert Hardy

did a feature on institutional racism in Liverpool in 1949 and took a series of pictures at Eva's home where she lived with her daughters and grandchildren. The pictures show a run-down Georgian house with damp and ripped wallpaper. Their clothes are coarse, old, and dirty. There's one shot of a bedroom in which you can count five beds.

The one that fascinates me most is taken in the kitchen. There's Eva by the stove, bending forward tending to one of the children, there's other children and one of her daughters milling about and a man (a son in law) sat at the table. What intrigues me most are the photographs, pictures and trinkets on the shelves in the photograph; more clues to knowing these figures, understanding their lives and their histories. I wonder who is in those pictures within the picture, Eva's father, or husband? If I zoom in enough, he looks smartly dressed and like he's holding something. Is it a drum? It's too blurry to make out. It fills me with so much wonder, what more is there to uncover just out of view?

I no longer feel like a little lost black girl who doesn't belong here. I've come to understand not only my personal heritage but the context in which it unfolded and, in that sense, I feel not only at home in Liverpool but part of the brickwork, its history, the fabric of its DNA. This fact doesn't fill me with a warm and fuzzy sense of belonging that I'd imagined either, but a complex mix of emotions. I love my city, I love being scouse, I love being black. Yet the facts are I'm a descendant of enslaved people, of poor white people, of post-industrial capitalism. Born and raised in a city that evolved from the profits of the Atlantic Slave Trade. Its an understanding that on the one hand affirms my sense of identity but on the other presents new ideas about who I am and what home is. But what I do know now for certain is that my roots in this country and in this city are generations deep. I understand the hardships and sadness my ancestors have overcome for me to be here at all, breathing, loving my children, typing stories. And I am eternally grateful.

Life in Our Home
Robert Burnett

What is our home?
A place of style and comfort.
A homage.
The place that keeps your dreams.

The place you fell in love with
the first time you saw it.
The place you spend time in
making it your very own.
The furnish,
The fittings; everything.
Everything you have.

A Home is for life,
for the people you leave behind.
To carry on with the home that you fell in love in.
To make a home is to live.

Love

Shalaw's Story
Shalaw

He is like a taxi every day, but on days when he is very sad to the point of coming out of his skin, he only goes to a place called the city square. When he gets there, he sits on the chair and lights a cigarette in his mind. Without realising what he is thinking, he picks up his violin and plays it. He cannot stop his tears.

As always, there is an old man with a long, white beard, eyebrows, deep eyes and young cheeks. He looks like the pictures in exhibitions. When he looks around, he hears the first note of the violin and recognises it. He stops, shakes his head a little, then slowly gets up and walks out of the pub, thinking about how these songs should be composed.

Haiku & Cinquains

A day
with nobody
changing my point of view
free my shackles
so I can see
a life.

Merrily zoning
in the light of my gloaming
I'm deeply toning.

I am a man, a captain
I like freedom
Thirty years old, a student.

One hard, hard concept I,
just cannot describe, cry out
clash of my mind, cry of heart.

When I started here
I did not see any hope there
later I see you.

I'm lost without you
if I search for you tomorrow
I will find you nowhere.

Midnight Tryst
Susan Goligher

Sun goes down
Silence all around
Softly floats the peel of the bell
Signalling that all will be well
Stealthily slipping into the room
Swinging around in a single glide
Steel flashing like a seductive smile
Stretching out two arms.

Securely held face to face
Strong arms supporting the hip
Spinning as they dance
Swaying to and fro circling around
Skilfully meander to the door
Sliding and gliding to a halt.

Swept up again
For one last dance
A pause as they take position
To gracefully restart their waltz
Slowly and softly whirling across the floor
As they float back around again
Then seated reluctantly on the edge of the bed.
They know their midnight tryst has come to an end.

Don't Give Up
A.S.

I do not know from where to start. I would like to share my experience with you because I want to change someone's life and their mindset to encourage them to seek help. Someone like you might find yourself in my experience, and really need to listen to what I'm going to say.

Like everyone else, I have been having a difficult time in my life. Things that you don't expect happen to us, happened to me. My life has changed a lot, and not for good. I was feeling weak, and my body could not move, feeling scared, my eyes were rounded, and my mouth opened wider. I felt my body tense and I was feeling angry with what happened that moment with me, but I felt I did not have the right to be angry and I was frightened. My body was shaking and sweating, my heart beating faster and my breathing was having difficulties. I could not move, and I was worried about myself. I was trembling, feeling weak and tired.

My anxiety started to take over my life. Living everyday with anxiety was horrible. I was feeling nervous for everything, my body was tense all the time and I was thinking something bad was going to happen to me. I was feeling hopeless and I could not find one reason why I would stay alive, why I would fight to be positive. I was thinking that life hadn't been fair with me. Then I was feeling worthless, I was thinking to harm myself, feeling down all the time. I lost pleasure for doing things that I used to like. I was feeling tired all the time. I could not concentrate, nor sleep. With even small things, I was getting angry, my face tensed up all the time and my eyebrow tightened. I could not think properly, was trying to avoid people, thinking that everyone wanted to harm me, I was thinking all the time negative things and that made me want to live in a dark tunnel.

I could not see what I've got. I could not value and appreciate things, and now I feel sad about that, my face is down, and my head goes down too. Then I sought help as I could not manage to live like that anymore and I'm so happy that I found the strength to ask for help because I was thinking it's a shame to do that, and my housemates would think I'm crazy. But things here are different and asking for help is the best thing you can do for yourself.

When I had my first counselling, the therapist recommended me to volunteer. I did not know where I found the strength to start volunteering, but I did. Firstly I started with A Better Tomorrow, then with British Red Cross. In the beginning it was enjoyable, and difficult at the same time. I was happy to start, excited, my face smiling and my cheeks rose up. I've got a chance to get out of the house which was helpful for my mental health.

While I was volunteering, I was hearing different problems and facing different people with different backgrounds. I was feeling sad for them and my head would go down and my face would look down too. I was trying to help them as much as I could, I was doing my best. I was helping asylum seekers and refugees with their needs, like with vaccinations during the pandemic. It was risky for me to meet with people because of covid, but I wanted to be there for them. To help the community, and to do good for others, it made me happy. When I saw the smile on their faces, I wanted to fly because of the happiness.

When I look back now this was a big change in my life. Since I decided to look after myself. I started to read books, watching Ted Talks on YouTube, have therapy, volunteering, helping myself to get out of the circle I was in and now I see a different person. I'm glad today I'm able to help myself first and others, look at things in the way they are and think differently. I'm still working hard on myself as I promised to take care of myself. If I do not do that no one is going to do the same for me. My face is smiling gnow and I'm showing my teeth.

It is difficult. It is not easy. I cannot forget what I have been through for a month. I cannot pretend either but now I'm saying to myself 'it's okay to have a bad time, not feeling well, but what's more important is: move on, don't give up.'

I think things happen for a reason and we are here for a reason, even though it was bad. I was sad, angry, wanting to scream, my head and face looking down. But I think there is a reason for that and today I want to study psychology. I want to know more about mental health to be a good psychologist and to help people, especially vulnerable people.

I want to tell you; life is not easy for everyone but please do not give up. Work hard on yourself, love, and respect yourself and most importantly accept yourself for who you really are. Live the life that you want to live, live for yourself, do not compare yourself with others. You must look after yourself, get better and have a better life. Life isn't that bad moment that happened to you, you are not a bad person, what has happened does not define you. You are a good person and deserve to be happy and to have a good life. Change the way of thinking and you will see how your life will change. Please help yourself and others as well, be kind to yourself and those around you. Don't take everything personally. Your mindset, like mine, might not change for one, two, or three months, but please keep working on yourself and you will be there.

I miss my golden old days when my mind was happy and peaceful and I'm still working hard to reach there. Do not forget it's you who are responsible for your life, your happiness.

Please be happy, loving and kind with yourself and others.

Take care.

Foolish Honour
Isaac Mendez

In a nightclub, I maintained my aloofness under
golden flecks of light that glistened in my whisky.
Suddenly, a brunette woman approached, gate crashing
my peace.
          'Where are you from?'
          'I am Nigerian.'
          'Wow,' she responded, her eyes travelled around
my face. 'I'm from Watford. Sadly, not as exotic as you...'
I was the bittersweet tang that slapped
her taste buds, signalling her fuzzy brain
to prolong an uncommon thrill
only I could provide.

A possibility of being discardable
Like sur milk spat out. It disrupted
an orthodox flavour that already
existed in her mouth.
She had branded me: OUTSIDER,
removing me form the crowd of tippling
bodies that blended my disguise.
With her tongue, she proclaimed her power.
          I was not authentic enough to initiate
          the tactile feel of glass clutched
          to her fingers. Tap,

tap,
tap. Her finger flitted
about to pluck
an exotic fruit.

I had embodied the vodka itself,
allowing her to decide whether she wanted
to see through
swallow
acknowledge the fact that
all the while, this liquid was *here.*

Mirror
Zareena Banu Abdul

Mirrors looking for the face,
to see the unseen emotions of a woman who hide the wall
of insecurity,
waiting for her valentine to walk hand in hand in the field
to vent the steam of pent up emotions
to feel the freedom touch her skin
to stare at the boundless sky
watching the swirling smoke of cigarette
The world opens around her when she left herself and
when you let her.

Music
Mohammed

Relax: it helps me Relax.
Dance: it helps me Dance.
Rap: it helps me Rap.
It helps me play football.
Let's have a good time listening to our favourite song.
I like American music; 50 Cent and The Game.
I love music.
It makes me happy.

I Am Zareena
Zareena Banu Abdul

I am made of gold
I am precious and rare
I am strong and hard
I can melt with enough heat
I am my mother's expectation and wait
I am my father's pride and content
I am a sister to look up to
I am a wife, adored galore
I am a peacock on a rainy day
I am a cuckoo singing everyday
I am a teacher to my toddler
I am a friend to my daughter
I am the sun to my family
I am the centre of gravity
I am the stage for my children
I am the audience for any reaction.

Maria
Maria Grace Rajani Antonydunstan

I am Maria, a mother of miracles
The one who bears great responsibility,
I am a leader of a family, the ladder of my children,
the loader of the food I provide.
I am a role model in my home, the one they look up to,
a peak of sacrifices made.
I am the reminder that Jesus died for our sins in Calvary
and carried a crushing cross,
whilst being beaten and bleeding.
Mother Mary, I have no idea how she was able to manage
the pain,
of her child dying in such a horrible way.
From the patience she held after the death of her son.
The world at the moment is in such a rush.
We quickly run after money, not noticing those that we
crush.
We need to slow down, and hold onto patience.
Please slow down and look at your neighbours.
Don't crush them on the way of your run,
Slow down, slow down!

Minion
Maria Grace Rajani Antonydunstan

Minion, three years ago, when I lay down on my bed, surprisingly, my son came home with you
from Russia.
In these three years, you were sleeping with me, staring at me, arguing with me when I lay down.
Because you were hanging in front of my bed.
I really liked the colour pink before.
Now I like blue and yellow, because of you.
You're my best friend now.
I am alone   I am frustrated   I am confused.
But I am still alive because of your big eyes, that look at me, when I lay down on my bed.
Nowadays, I really like to lay down on my bed, because I like your staring by, big eyes.
The eyes saying, he will come soon.

Love
Pauline Cummins

I loved you from the very start
With every beat of my gentle heart.
Miraculously healed over the years
Brave and resolutely overcoming fears.

Emotional barriers moved aside
Dispelling viewpoints once my guide.
Finally escaping the deep black-hole
That'd withheld myself from my very soul.

Distrustful thoughts had sealed my fate
Until courage became my new dictate.
Protecting my heart as if it were a shrine
Now rising to claim what's rightfully mine.

Allowing love to envelop my being.
Realising a joyful state was freeing
Promising to love you with all of my heart
Knowing even in death, we'll never part.

Journeys

Journey on a Train
Robert Burnett

Business bodies mixed with the holiday crowd gathered at
the station.
Mothers needing eyes in the back of their heads to keep
control of their children.

We board; packed like sardines.
The whistle blows and we're off,
jampacked for hours.

We journey through the hot and stuff carriages of the
train,
Cramped, through the harsh lands of people.
Some old, some not so old
The youngest at the back.

Children are wide eyed, noses to the window,
straining to see the beach,
They dream of the sun on their backs,
the fair,
the sand under their grubby hands.

We should all be like them.
Like excited children on a trip to the beach.

Give life a chance and be yourself.
Just like the ocean.

The Texture of Silence

Sometimes, we discuss the taste
of the night in our mouths.
In this open house given to us,
light never crawls in.

A crippling shiver has seized
our knees.
So, we stay put, joined together
like knitted sardines.

We have forgotten our eyes
and pretend to clap at mosquitoes,
so we know who comes through
the cryptic door.

When our hands don't meet,
we join palms and pray that our ears
catch the last crying echo of
the voice we cannot remember.

Nomads of the Desert
Robert Burnett

Yellow strains of golden sand stretch as far as the eye can
see.
Large black eagles soar wild and free, roaming the tinted
blue sky.
Camels line the caravans for miles and miles.

The Nomad tribe's people trade their worthy goods.
Later, they pitch their large tents and cook, eat, share
stories of the desert,
of roaming the landscape with their children,
their way of life for years and years.

In their mouths they hold their destiny
and the names of ancient places.
They claim the earth.
Their legacy will always remain.

Crossing Borders

Immigration: From Eritrea to UK
Okubat Tesfaldet

My name is Okubat and I was born in Arawti near Areza in the debub or southern region of Eritrea. The events of my short life illustrate why so many Eritreans are fleeing the country.

I was crossing the border to Ethiopia alone at night with only a stick to protect myself against the hyena lions and the military squads who pick up runaways. It was tiring but I could not stop.

I was risking my life to get out of Eritrea so I could have freedom. Eritrea is one of the most repressive countries in the world where young people have no future. Their choice is to undertake compulsory national service or try to flee Eritrea. National service is harsh, pays a pittance and goes on indefinitely. Usually, conscripts to go into the military.

I was not asked about my education. I discontinued my education when I was in Grade 10 as the authorities arrested me from school and took me to the main country prison near Barentu in February 2014. My father had been detained over five years. Therefore, I was arrested and detained for seven months.

I was tortured in detention. My teeth were broken when I was beaten up with a metal object. After being released around September 2014. I was sent to do military training at Shakat near Barentu. I fled national service around the end of 2014.

Every month thousands of young people like me sneak out of the country, ending up in Sudan, Libya and Europe, or dying along the way.

The Story of 10 Days Traveling
Altiab Awad

I didn't know travelling through smuggling was so difficult
until I tried it.
Last year I started my journey from city to city.
The smugglers treated us like slaves.
In that 10 days I didn't eat more than 5 meals, I was hungry
and near death.
They took us to camp.
In the camp there is too many people.
Imagine.
They hit people with weapons without any reason.
They hit numbers of people to scare the rest.
What I saw there was suffering; children, families.
I have a strong memory of it all.
On the first day when I arrived to that camp, I saw them
hitting people, a man, without a shiver of blood.
He was saying *please please please stop*.
They were devoid of feelings.

I saw a wife and husband suffer.
Every night we stood in line for counting and they chose a
group of us to travel.
On the last day they made us wait in line on our knees.
They called us out, one after the other.
They called the wife and husband.

She was cursing but there was nothing she could do because she couldn't stand up.
We had been on our knees for more than two hours.

I didn't know travelling through smuggling was so difficult until I tried it.

Guymana
Altiab Awad

I left Guymana at the age of four,
So I was told; I don't remember those days.
I grew up in a place with no close relatives, only some
wonderful neighbours.
I wondered why we were alone.

My mother told me stories of her younger years,
before the problems started that forced my family to leave.
Fire.
Smoke.
Ash.
Our home burned.

We had a black donkey, our entire life loaded onto his back,
including my two sisters.
My mother and older sister walked and my mother carried
me.
What a difficult time.
My grandfather, old and unable to walk; was killed.
My mother told me our home is now a graveyard.

We went to my father and I grew up in a new place.
The war followed us,
claimed my village and father.

Fire.
Smoke.
Ash.
Our new home burned…
But I did not.

A camp for the displaced in the city of Nyala.
We lived a heavy life.
I toiled to provide for my family, just like my father before
me.
The truest man I ever met.
He taught me to learn, let go.
Don't stand idly by.
Fire.
Smoke.
Ash.
My new home can't burn.

We can't change the past, but we can learn from it.

I left Libya.
When I arrived in Europe I felt safe for the first time.
SAFE – if the world becomes unsafe where shall we go?
Fire.
Smoke.
Ash.
To be human is to have humanity.
The world can't burn.

Shukri's Story
Shukri Mohammed

Once upon a time a little girl fled a genocide. She witnessed horrific horrendous crimes. She was haunted by the memories of her people being murdered. She lost family. She witnessed what no child should witness; her family killed, their blood, their bodies.

She started a new life in Liverpool as a child of 9 years old, to be reunited with her father, and siblings she never met before. She was excited about her new life and had long dreamed about her father who she had met twice.

In her dreams she did not see what would be hardest of all, to come to a country where you don't speak the language, can't communicate with your siblings and are put to school. Teachers speaking to you, children speaking to you but you not understanding what they are saying.

In her dreams she did not see the racism and discrimination she would face in British society. Being chased by skinheads. A child assaulted by a grown man because of her skin. A man, with a dog and tattoos and a baseball bat, shouting 'oi niggers, oi you fucking black … come back here!' and not understanding. Fleeing from genocide to come to the land of peace to experience racism.

The little girl is me and how I missed my mother and motherlands. I was for a long time desperate to go back.

The Product of Colonisation
Claire Beerjeraz

Where would I be without the culture of my life
If I chose to turn away and formed a blind eye
That's what they expected
If you resided in this country
A perceptive translation
All the power and control
Made with false promises no accusations
Instilling all the worth down to the soil of the ground
The same one you indirectly helped grow
From the people to the land
But don't hesitate or stutter
Or be shocked or hold breathless mutters
Because when I reflect on trades that were made
The unlawful depiction of what was meant to be great
I understand, conquered, saw, and became
Your product of colonisation in this game

Although the fast-paced glances
And excessive overtness seems reduced
The smell of appropriation and control
Still lingers through my roots
I question where to reside
Where I belong
And who will listen

All distinct but linked
I am still the product of colonisation

That universal understanding of the carrot and the stick
A performative and theatrical
Action to constrict
It draws you in then pulls you back
The silence felt as it winds and wraps
Around your throat
Don't speak don't touch
The product of colonisation has no real meaning to us

Perception is real
But I don't know how to feel
When they ask me who's tradition is this?
It feels confrontational
Because I can't not be irate
When I think about all the things that have been stolen
and faked
Museums never-ending full of items that once belonged to
another
Never to be returned or acknowledged for that matter
Democracy means that we actually have no say
If you're part of the Windrush generation
Even your own identity may not get to stay
But please keep it down
Don't make a big deal

The only thing you'll evoke is a dismissal of this rift
The product of colonisation doesn't exist

'No offence but...'
Mmm No, I think I will end up being offended
They move with such engagement
I can taste the slithered sounds
Of the piercing jabs from their tongues
As they minimise our experiences first hand
My art is taken, turned away or denied
Too confrontational and uncomfortable for your narrow
mind
I am grateful for my life
But that doesn't take away
From the constant reminder of how I was made
The floors I move on, the resources I take in
Are depictions of the past and current crimes that are and
have been
Modern slavery hidden under laws
Racism and sexism minimised by telling us there isn't a
war
But there are many
physically, emotionally, and mentally
Locally, universally in its entirety
Pause.
But there are many
physically, emotionally, and mentally

Locally, universally in its entirety... Pause.
Don't we have an arms deal?
The product of colonisation is showcasing as real

We gaze at the trope of being the most woke
let's look around and start at your home
The media consumed with a white haze
Tells you it's black vs. White
We just want to be treated the same
Our traits and looks praised in whiteness
Once dehumanised for the very same thing
Trying to re-empower ourselves
That's all we want to bring

The product of colonisation
Speaks up again
But will the product of colonisation
Have their rights in the end?

The Struggle Goes On

Mandela 8 March
Isaac Mendez

"I have fought against white domination, and I have fought against black domination. I have cherished the ideal of a democratic and free society in which all persons live together in harmony with equal opportunities. It is an ideal which I hope to live for and to achieve. But if needs be, it is an ideal for which I am prepared to die for."
Nelson Mandela

On the morning of the march, I was interviewed by a young woman from Liverpool. Before then, I could tell she was curious about something because she spent a while roaming around the premises, vanishing behind the back of placards and group chatter when I caught her demeanour. I was summoned by Madeline, one of the project leaders.

'When we start the march, you and Kasey will be in the front carrying the *Black Organisation* banner, if that's fine? Then when we get to the boulevard, the Apartheid banner will replace you guys from the back,' she says.

'Sure, I don't mind that.'

I trekked towards the drummers and dancers dressed in black tights and bright yellow cotton ribbons. I wanted to get a water bottle when the interviewer finally seized her moment.

'Excuse me, is it alright if I ask you a few questions?' she said, joining her hands together as if she was praying for my cooperation. She looked gleeful, as though she had an assurance that I was to be the right man with the right answers.

Interviewer: what's happening here, and what is your role in all this?

I am only a volunteer. Today we are marching to Princes Park in celebration of the achievement of Nelson Mandela. The entire project is called the Mandela8.

Interviewer: What are these achievements you speak of, and what does it mean to you?

There is only so much I can tell you about the man from Mvezo. Imagine dedicating your entire life to equality and dismantling racial oppression, that you were imprisoned. Even more so, accepted the possibility of death. Mandela makes me believe that immortality is achievable. Look at us, a young, scouse woman seeking the opinion of a Nigerian. Look at the drummers and volunteers all wearing smiles and carrying different skin tones, willing to represent each other in the celebration of somebody unrelated to their bloodline. It's so beautiful it could make you cry in your sleep. This is a rendition of the vision of a great man, don't you think? I see myself as an activist, you know. And although the fight for equality is not entirely won, this sure makes me want to dream.

Great Peace Must Come
Altiab Awad

I discussed peace with a number of people recently, to find out what they think. The last person I asked, he said, 'I am certain there will be no complete peace.'

My personal view: there will be world peace, it just takes courage.

The optimism we dream of, a vision emerging before us. The end of flight, the establishment of international cooperation through the bodies, and agencies that are formed for this purpose. This is only a stage of the necessary stages for existence. To avoid nuclear massacre, peace will only be achieved in the union of the people in the world as one global family.

There are some detractors, such as racial discrimination, which is one of the most harmful evils. A true obstacle to peace. Working within these principles is a flagrant violation of dignity, and it can't be accepted with any excuse.

Social discrimination hinders those who are under its fire. It also corrupts those who practice it, and distrupts human progress and advancement.

At the beginning of the peace phase, we must find appropriate diplomatic solutions to stop wars all over the world, we have to make peace our only goal and we have to strive for it together.

We will definitely achieve it.

We must say 'no' to conflict and fanaticism and bloodshed.

We must say 'welcome' to peace and tolerance and 'welcome' to solidarity and love.

These useless conflicts will cease, and these destructive wars will be extinguished, by permission of the Creator.

Great peace must come.

Yemen: The Elephant in the Room
Pariah Miah

The world watched
...and we did nothing
Because we didn't create the problem?
Or we didn't have the time!
Conditioned to feel powerless
But we knew at our core
That we are the majority
We should have done more
Imagine for a moment...
It was us...our children, suffering in this senseless war.

War Game
Pariah Miah

If you must treat war like a game, let war be a battle of wit
and intellect, reason and rational.
What are you afraid of?
Bring to the table, your plans, show the world your hand.
Death is not an option, neither is oppression.
What are you afraid of?
If chess be your game, by all means be the King.
May your bishop be wise, may your knight be brave.
Your rook will be swift and your Queen courageous.
What are you afraid of?
And when you sacrifice your pawns, made of ebony and
gold, you will be sparing the lives of our youth, who had
dreams of getting old.
What are you afraid of?

Microaggressions

Notoriously difficult to articulate,
nothing was said, there was no debate.
Just a piercing swift glance of hate,
by those who fixate and choose to slate.
Those who's beauty are displayed in shades
of midnight brown and elaborate braids.
Skins of bronze and cinnamon brown,
of a depth and breadth that spellbound.
Beautiful tonal degrees of colour
So different from their own pale pallor.

Their nonverbal aggressions,
another weapon of oppression.
Relentless and cruel,
a silent deadly tool.
To keep us in our place
As they Invade our personal space.
By those seething inside,
as they bide their time.
To the moment and place
they can intimidate.

Powered by self-righteousness,
a perceived sense of entitlement.
Feelings of supremacy

a belief in their superiority.
With no or little empathy,
for those looking differently.
Tired of being distraught,
as they exhibit no remorse.
Their unwarranted aggression,
just another transgression.

Structurally excluded
within organisations they collude- in.
Hitting the glass ceiling
as they remain unyielding.
Bored of their insensitivity,
unfathomable idiosyncrasies.
The monotonous debate
about whether they can relate.
According to the bigger picture
we're equal says, the holy scripture.

No longer waiting for equality,
or equal opportunity.
Tired of racist assumptions,
stereotypes and presumptions.
Deliberately marginalised,
By those they call civilised.
As they protect their interests,
Whilst, feathering their own nests.

Misappropriating our culture,
as they circle us, like vultures

Racial gaslighting, another game,
bending reality to their own gain.
Despite knowing we're all the same.
Stakes are high in this elaborate game.
Mental control the ultimate goal,
another form of social control.
Despite their anti-racist training
their unconscious bias, isn't waning.
Exhausted with the same old rhetoric
as they demonstrate no moral ethics.

No longer allowing you to throw us off track,
with your covert sniper attacks.
With facial expressions and critical looks,
their taunt body postures we can't overlook.

The hyper vigilant are on the move for we have nothing
left to prove.
It's time for them to 'Take the knee' and bow their head
before me.

The Uprising of 1981
Pauline Cummins

Sustained attacks and false arrests
came the uprisings and unrest
Tactical policing with little respect
Policies planned for maximum effect
extreme force and headlocks
body blows and handcuffs.
Willfully criminalising our teens
Lives destroyed with undreamt dreams
The burden of proof lay with us
To prove the police hurt our youth
Lawless, armed with CS canisters,
tactics more akin to gangsters.
The resourceful fought and won the cruel
Bringing an end to Ken Oxford's rule.
The uprising on that fateful day
Turned the course of history
The brave fought and won the conceited
the police found themselves defeated
Soon after, the defence committee was formed
out of which the Law Centre was born
to monitor the police and judiciary
Providing representation when necessary.

The human cost has been too great

in our home known as Liverpool 8.
Lives taken while others left early
all are remembered to us dearly.
Many fought to life's last breath
But we will all be reunited at our death.
The brave who walked before
Have left their imprint upon us all.
Many organisations have campaigned
to bring about lasting change.
As the League of Coloured People before
When anti-black race riots erupted in seaports
Liverpool's steeped in the blood of slaves
forced and shipped across the waves
Liverpool city was built on this trade
The truth it will take it to its very grave.
Still in the past
Liverpool has held steadfast
To political structures and infrastructures
Which have tried to hold us back
But we've come too far and remain on track.

Knowing that racism is socially constructed
man-made by the obstructive
keeping their power through educational and
governmental structures
Our history is steeped in nobility like the great African
kingdoms of antiquity

We are standing tall with dignity
as we take a quantum leap towards our destiny.

Enslaved
Claire Beerjeraz

What was it like when they unearthed you from this
country?
Did they encase you in resin, to keep you preserved?
Or hang you in museums to pretend *you're* there for them
to learn?
I ponder if they treated you as real,
A breathing human being with the ability to feel.
Was it hard,
To not cut your roots, because they made you believe your
culture should be pruned
Or question your authenticity just because they could?
Was it hard to live?
Ha…
That was a silly question.
You knew it was better to exist, you learnt that the hard
way.
They would take sips of your coffee-coloured skin and
would spit it at the walls.
Your energy too warm,
Taste too naïve,
Undertones of a native-tongue that felt so bitter-sweet.
You had never seen snow,
 So you wore flipflops to the store

You went from bread but came back with sourdough
soaked in salty tear,
Feet coloured like a black forest cherry,
And hands blue like the pigment in our flag.
But was it Red, White and Blue, or Red, Blue, Yellow and
Green?
The choice was yours but...
String dangled from your arms like silk spun webs,
Cues in the background of what you *should* have said.
'Britons shall never never be slaves'
Yet you stood there,
Passport in hand
Confused...
Muddled as to why you felt like that...
Why you felt enslaved.

What You Gonna Say?
Reuben Williams

Call me every name under the sun,
What you gonna say to me now?
What you gonna do to hurt me now?
When my armour is on, you can't hurt me now.
Even if you could admit you were wrong
The damage is already done,
You can't reverse it now,
Why you gotta try and bring me down,
Soon you see karma come back around
Why do you feel you gotta snake and snitch?
Voodoo! Voodoo!
Voodoo! Voodoo!
You got me sticking pins in the poppet,
Do you feel that, snitch?
Jab! Jab!
I call on Baron Samedi & Maman Brigitte.
Voodoo! Voodoo!
You done messed with the wrong witch.

Call me every name under the sun,
What you gonna say to me now?
What you gonna do to hurt me now?
When my armour is on, you can't hurt me now.
Even if you could admit you were wrong

The damage is already done,
You can't reverse it now,
Why you gotta bring me down,
Soon you see karma come back around
Why does your mouth run a marathon whenever you
speak?
EGO! EGO!
You can't hold a candle next to me,
You feel the need to share your opinion on everything,
When your words are meaningless to me,
You're ignorant and arrogant,
Why do you think you've got authority over me?
EGO! EGO!
It must be, EGO! EGO!
You ain't got shit on me.
What you gonna say?
Say? Say?
What you gonna say?
Now the bridge is burnt.
Say? Say? Say?
WHAT YOU GONNA SAY?!

Call me every name under the sun,
What you gonna say to me now?
What you gonna do to hurt me now?
Even if you could admit you were wrong
The damage is already done,

You can't reverse it now,
Why you gotta try and bring me down,
Soon you see karma come back around
What you gonna say?
What you gonna say?
What you gonna say?
NOW.

The Television

Into a vortex we were thrown and caught.
Mindless and detached from all thought
Satellite or cable, we don't really care.
Glued to the screen as we sit and stare

Distracted by reality and talk shows galore
Pollical broadcasting biased at its core
Thrillers excite whilst rom-coms delight.
political campaigns persuade with their might.

Box sets stimulate so we constantly crave
Medicated on dopamine we're enslaved
Repetitive adverts bombard with hard-sells
Using psychology, we fall under their spell

Engulfing our lives in its entirety
Charmed and tricked by a false reality.
Changing our biology, it causes depression.
Creating and promoting cognitive regression.

Innocently inviting the television into our lives.
A powerful tool that constantly strives
to sell, entertain and spread the views
of those in power through the news.

Debt
Pauline Cummins

Drowning beneath the weight of debt
barely coming up for breath.
Unpaid bills in bold red print,
followed by threats of enforcement.

Forced to choose between food or fuel,
the sixth richest nation makes this cruel.
Four million children in poverty
making a mockery of equality.

Keeping children warm through the day
Piling on clothes to keep the cold at bay
Going without food so children can eat
Never being able to give them a treat.

The cost of livings going up in price
Keeping doors shut and switching off lights
Blocking out drafts to keep out chills.
Still never in a position to pay all the bills.

Poorly paid jobs, make it hard to survive.
The minimum wage needs to rise.
Poor quality housing with mould and spores
Causing allergic reactions behind closed doors.

Who knew life would be such a struggle
Despite loving our children it's one big hustle
Searching for bargains on the way to the till
Life is a continuous trudge up hill.

The Capitalist model is causing us pain.
Wealth for the few, the rest kept chained
Unforeseen cost and spiralling debt.
It's deliberate and not because we're inept.

Time for change, showing Capitalism the door
Where not permitting poverty anymore.
It only exits, because we allow it to be,
It's now time for justice and equality.

Keep on Moving

My Life
Florianne

I like my life because it's a story.
A single mother; happy to take care of her children alone.
My children are my world,
my first family.
I love them.
Swimming allows me to entertain myself.
The water dance helps me to explore my mind.
The gym helps me to relax.
Music softens moral.
I like writing, I feel good writing.
I like my life because it's a story.

One Small Step
Susan Goligher

Neil has nothing on me
With my fly NHS technology
I've been steppin' with my craft
And have made my own history
Up in the air above the clouds
Neil had to go to step out
Out of the ward along the corridor I went
To find out what the fuss was about.
My capsule was a wheelchair
Moon surface on the floor
My space rover a simulator walker
Who could want for more?
Just one small step Neil took
Up upon the moon
In my super-duper fly Arlo walker
I took loads more to my room.

This Is Me!
Dawn Paisley Mills

Exactly who you see
This is me.
The one they call crazy
But I ain't crazy
And I ain't lazy
My memory certainly
ain't hazy
I'm Amazing.

This is me
Temperamental just like the sea
I wanna be
somebody
And sometimes nobody
Unapologetic
Energetic
Seriously
I have no room for Jealousy

You see.
This is me

Tall like a tree
I can start fights with me
And I can set myself free
I ain't no mystery.
I'm consistent
you see
I'm feisty
I'm 90 years old
But I'm only 3
I refuse to face reality
I climb up walls defiantly
You see, this is me.

You see this is me
I sting like a bee
Like Our Father, show Mercy
Brave like Percy, fight like Trinity.
I am my blue Jersey
This is me.
You can follow and unfollow me
I have my own Destiny
Don't you be testing me
Police arresting me
Boyfriend caressing me

Children stressing me.
But I keep on dressing me
I always show up
for me
Can you see what the mandem see
When they're attracted to me.

This is me
I'm black like tea
No Nerves, Not Me!
I give generously
Want an A, Not a C
Will you be there for me
Cos This Is Me!

This is me
I ain't lowdown and dirty
I am decent, flirty but
show me courtesy
Just like her majesty
Travesty upon travesty
Please, show honesty
Stop pushing and pulling me
Telling your lies

Is my blackness affecting me?
Its rooted deep within
Sticks and stones
Are not hurting me
I am comfortable in my skin.

The name calling hardens me
I refuse to drown in the
Because This is me.

This is me
I don't scare, oh so easily!
Racist skinheads kept teasing me constantly
My big sister defends and takes care of me
She threw down, beat them up, and was there for me
Walk to school, play it cool, who's the fool?
It ain't me!

I fall down, get back up
This is me; you see!
Hold me close, drink a toast
Raise your glass towards me
Don't be shy, don't you cry
Don't forget, what you see

This is me, I am free
This is all of me.

Someone told me, that I must get over me
Don't forget, what you get
You get what you see
I will love you for all our eternity
I don't bend, I don't break
Wont bow down on my bended me
This is me; this is me!
This is me!

Once Upon A Time in Warribee

(Prologue)

Circa 1984, Aussie newspapers are harping on about Kiwi dole
bludgers arriving en masse - sunning themselves
on Sydney's beaches & taking advantage of the
reciprocal social care arrangements between the
two ANZAC nations.
NZ Prime Minister Rob MULDOON (following constant,
persistent midering) is pressed to respond:
"...this emigration has resulted in a situation which serves both
countries & is of mutually benefit. Clearly it has
*RAISED the AVERAGE **IQ** of BOTH*
COUNTRIES."

ANZAC: *acronym **Australian and New Zealand Army***
***Corps**. On the 25th of April 1915, Australian*
and New Zealand soldiers formed part of the
allied expedition that set out to capture the
Gallipoli peninsula. These became known as
Anzacs and the pride they took in that name
continues to this day.
Mider: *verb. (Northern England) **To make an unnecessary***
***fuss, moan, bother**. To pester or irritate*
someone.

This fella was reckoning. Mmm...how do I spend my day off? It was Saturday 8am.

Bloke can't help but rise early, regardless which day of the week. Most days start at 6. Get up, drive to depot. Park up in yard. Then up & out, onto the high-sided waste collection trucks. Get all the household rubbish from the good citizens' suburbs of West Melbourne.

Bruce loved his work: running all day, the other fellas never even had step off the tray at back-a-truck. Bruce'd run all day long, throwing bag after bag skilfully over the steep side walls of lorry, even from afar.

Never ever did he fail the shot. Well, hardly ever. All, but once. The oddity – one occasion he overshot the truck and the bag sailed out – on and on a little too much. Out, into oncoming traffic. Fortunately, the flaw wasn't fatal. Unfortunately, he'd hoped it'd become long forgotten. But this kiwi could hope on till the cows came home.

His Aussie workmates held sway – he was outnumbered. No chance! Fair Dinkum mate! Stone the crows! Like a bunch of drunk galahs, day in day out. Clock in to clock out, they'd cajole & cackle. Inflaming Bruce like a wild outta' control bushfire – yet he never let the irritation come to surface. He couldn't – the likely response would only be them turning up the heat...all that then coming to a fine head - before exploding out into an all-out toxic brawl...consequentially, leaving him without means to a daily keep.

A joker forever destined to be ribbed daily by his bastard colleagues – huh! Oh Ockers, such refined & able comedians, eh? Yeah right. Fuckin' Australians...still they can't help themselves & to think these were the best of the bunch: After all, Melbourne - is Aussie's self-proclaimed Capital of Culture. (From growing up, Bruce would recall his dear Mother's voice echoing into the present. Whenever it arose that he started to let pride get ahead of himself...he'd pull himself back to earth, sharpish.

'Listen here son - self-praise is no kinda recommendation').

Bruce the kiwi loved his job – hated Australians – but liked Australia.

Besides, living here was akin to virtue development (& hell was it much required!) – The virtue of patience.

A tolerance of obnoxious, & often bigoted roughnecks.

Today, well he'd take in a big leisurely breakfast. Then watch some footy. Something will be on...with a stroke of luck – It'd be New Zealand's All Blacks thumping the Australian Wallabies.

And maybe, just maybe with some much overdue - long time a coming luck...

A chance of a chat up, with some Fair Dinkum Aussie Sheilagh.

Keep developing those virtues then, eh mate.

Music In My Life
Jasmine Monthe

I like music in my life.

It sings softly,
conveys the things of life.
It soothes my heart
helps me forget my past love stories.

Music reminds me of my husband.
I dance when it sings,
listening in work and travel.

Religious music helps me in the word of God,
motivates me to prayer.
It softens moral and lifts my Christian life.

It helps me with depression.

What Cricket Means to Me
Sampath Siriwardena

Sri Lanka vs England 1982
(2ⁿᵈ One Day International)

I was twelve years old. It was my first time seeing a foreign cricket team; the England team. It was tropical hot. The Sri Lankan President and a few Cabinet Ministers were in attendance. The whole country was shut down, most of them glued in front of their televisions.

Our family and friends were together. It was really nice, enjoyable, laughing and chit chatting. We were whisked away by the person who came to pick us up. While travelling to the ground, we were singing as everybody was excited! The sooner we got there, the better.

We were thrilled!

The crowd was roaring. A nice cool breeze tickled my neck, sunshine and the clear blue sky made the day beautiful. Both teams were warming up on the ground, throwing the ball, swinging the bat, exercising as well.

Two umpires and both captains walked to the pitch and tossed a coin to decide the batters and fielders. The coin went up and down as the crowd held their breath. Who will bat and who will field? England won the toss and decided to field. Almost 22,000 spectators had gathered to watch the 2ⁿᵈ One Day International held on 14ᵗʰ February 1982.

People were cheering and signing and there were a few local music bands who encouraged the Sri Lankan cricket team. There were a sizable number of British Nationals too, the Sri Lankan captain was Bandula Warnapura and the England captain was Keith Fletcher.

Bandula Warnapura was caught and balled by Ian Botham. Next came Sidath Wettimung, who scored a brilliant knockout of 86 runs, lifted the score together with Roy Dias. Arjura Ranathunga was the youngest player to be in the Sri Lankan side, while studying at school he scored a classic 42 runs. John Lever bowled fantastically, taking a few wickets.

The atmosphere was electric on the grounds, it was bright and sunny with a cool breeze. Thrilled fans we moving around the boundary with a national flag, sooner a player played with a six of a four. The rest of the players couldn't make better scores and at the end of the overs Sri Lanka was at 215/7 at the close of play (45 overs).

We had a nice break for lunch and evening tea. My Mum and Dad and their friends bought the meal. There were patriotic music, Sri Lankan and English songs too.

England started batting with Gooch and Cook which put England in a strong position with a partnership of 109 runs. Cook was dismissed as England's first wicket and lost their second and third wickets at close intervals.

England had to score 14 runs in the last two overs. As a result, the English players wants to score quickly, they lost

6th, 7th and 8th wickets with quick run outs. With two balls remaining, Bob Willis hit the ball high in the air and was caught by Ranjan Madugalla.

Finally, the match ended with a victory for Sri Lanka! Jubilant spectators tried to rush the ground to hug the players, but police prevented it from happening. Some Sri Lankan fans ran to the England team to get their autographs signed.

The Sri Lankan President made a speech congratulating both teams, especially praising the Sri Lankan cricket team for their magnificent performance and gave away the prizes for the England cricket team and for the winning Sri Lankan team.

The whole crowd were cheering, singing and some were dancing too. It was a historic match, which Sri Lanka won after getting test status.

On the way home people were waving Sri Lankan flags and lighting crackers on the streets. Our family arrived home before dusk. The match dominated the television, radio, and news. Me and my friends stayed outside on the road, talking about the match late into the night. I realised I had to go home when I heard my Mom and Dad shout at me for being late for my dinner!

The Sri Lanka Vs England 2nd One Day match was an exciting, thrilling game.

I started my cricket career when I was around nine years old for my primary school team with a leather ball; but before that I used to play cricket with a soft ball and bat with my family and friends. Cricket has been that much embodied to my soul. It is the most famous game in Sri Lanka (even though it's not the national game, which is volleyball.)

I became the all-island best cricket bowler in the same year (1982) in my high school.

Almost four decades have gone now. I feel always cricket is in my blood and is engraved on my body. There is a quote 'Cricket is a gentleman's game.'

Cricket was founded by the English and it has spread to the whole world. I feel cricket is a medicine to unify the nations and put a smile on the face of all human beings.

Twelve
Dawn Paisley Mills

When I was twelve years old, my mum took me and my brothers and sisters to the social services building and left us there. My mum had finally run out of options, after being thrown out of the Salvation Army Hostel for battered wives for beating up the red-faced staff member Anne, and her colleague, for calling us monkeys.

We were then transported to a filthy skanky, 'Rising Damp' type women's hostel, called Marsh Lane. That was so uninhabitable we only stayed one night. My Mum and all seven of us sharing the one dirty double bed, three at the bottom and four at the top with Mum. The topic of conversation all night was the smashed window with the dirty sock stuffed inside of it to stop the draught. Mum was in hysterics all night laughing at that. We hardly got any sleep because we scorned the filthy, holed up, stained up, itchy flea bitten blankets all night and didn't want them to touch our skin. Mum continued to laugh all night about us looking down upon our situation. Although we didn't know she had already made up her mind about what her next move was.

She gave away most of her beautiful 70s clothes to the poor, downtrodden women in Marsh Lane. I remember trying on her brown suede tassel jacket and her rainbow knitted hot pants before they were all bagged. Next, we got a taxi to the social services building where I observed my Mum talking with our male Social Worker (the goggle-eyed *Where's Wally?* lookalike Mr Saunders, nicknamed Soggy by all the Mums he worked with). I observed him with his thick glasses and the almost lecherous way that he stared at Mum.

Mum was sitting opposite Soggy in his office as he pleaded with her not to do this.

'Please don't do this,' he begged.

But she laughed like a teenage girl and told him she couldn't help it. Next, she left to go to the shop next door and buy six packets of crisps and handed them all out to her six children. We were shown a box of toys by Mr Saunders' assistant, and we could keep them, and I was so happy with my purse, filled with new handkerchiefs.

I then saw my Mum leave the building and as I looked out of the huge windows of the social services, I saw my Mum getting on the back of our married stepdad's motorbike and riding off into the Sunset! I remember then being driven to a children's home in the racist part of town called Seacroft. The boys were put in a separate home and we girls were kept together. When we arrived at the children's home, we were greeted by the aunties, as they liked to be called and they sent two of the boys in the home to buy pork pies for our dinner: the worst meal ever, pork pie with hard sweet peas out of the can. I still can't eat pork pies or tinned peas to this day. We were then shown to our dorm room which contained four clean beds and was beautiful. Easdale Crescent children's home was beautiful and clean.

My first day of school was full of surprises.

As I made my way across the school grounds, 'HEY NIGGA, HEY NIGGA' was shouted.

I'd heard this word before, used at my old school but the word still stung twelve-year-old me. A few weeks later, as I was taking my six-year-old sister to school accompanied by one of the boys from our children's home, we became aware that we were being followed so we quickened our steps, and so did the two white boys behind us hellbent on trouble that morning!

At first I tried to ignore the boys as they came right up behind us making racist comments, but it soon became apparent that ignorance is not bliss, as they got so close behind me that they were stepping on the backs of my shoes and then began pushing me. I was scared and hoped they would leave us alone, but the more I ignored them, the worse they became until I had no choice but to turn around to ask them to stop. Big mistake. This was like a red rag to a bull and as I turned round, he was straight in my face attacking me. Next, we are both on the ground, the blonde-haired skinhead was on top of me - like two grown men in a bar room brawl. I didn't know what to do as we both rolled down the hill, him on top of me, then me on top of him. He was shouting 'come on nigga' in my face as we rolled and fought. I had long nails back then and it suddenly came to me to scratch his eyes out during a ' fight or flight' moment of madness. I heard him scream as I dug deep into his flesh and then he rolled off of me clutching his face tightly as his friend backed away in horror.

I stood up and realised I'd won the fight in amazement. His friend backed away from me and stood over his screaming friend. I took hold of my sister's hand and took her to school proud and smug and delighted that I'd won that fight in her presence.

Had I lost, who knows what he would've done to her. After that he always said hi to me at school.

I Have To Be Somewhere

I Am a Deep, Dark Sea

I am a deep, dark sea
between the restless surface and the calm bottom
I wander
keeping still may save you
but flowing will enliven you!
Yes, you exist. But what if you disappear?
Yes, you are existing. But what if you just disappear?

This might not all be true
but I have to be somewhere,
don't I?
A flamingo isn't born
with pink feathers anyway
they nest on hot sand
my cigarette is a punctuation mark.

The life doesn't have a price
when you want to become successful in life.
You have to work hard
and focus on something that you know better.
Push yourself, for your dreams.

I am an empty half-house.
You can find me in a Yemeni teacup
caught between mother's tongue
and a British flag.
I feel drowned between two homes.

The Flying Land
Eman

Eleven years is my timeline,
born on the Tahir square.
Fled the Rabaa massacre.
We were the first loved people,
then we vanished.
The moment when we reunited with family,
now we are separated.
Friends who marked their words on the flying flag,
now on the rock walls of the prison cells.
When the Military interfered .

I used to live, now I am nowhere.
It feels like I have no roots,
or my roots have been cut out.
An Egyptian tragic story,
to Qatari expat, to a British immigrant.
I am a Bedouin.
I tried to live in many places to find home,
but I am still searching.

I was a dreamer, but reality was upon me.
I know we can't change it,
but we can evoke the sound of it.

I don't know where I am.
I am just a memorial.
My ties were cut out so I can breathe,
to find new friends, to find a new home, to start again.
But the fingerprints still mark on me,
will they ever be removed?

I smell dust, pain, and blood.
I smell black pepper.

I can hear chants.
I am the friend of those who ink on my skin
Two lovers whisper,
I hear cracks of feet,
escaping the square.

I feel I can't wrap my arms around the loved one,
but their voices still awake me.

You left your mark on me.
You printed on me.
Between the prison Walls,
we still speak to each other.
Isn't it ironic?
You are here, but I can longer see you, feel you.

If I was to return,

I would reunite with my friends
to remember you.

But those who mark you,
even those who are no longer here.
Some of those who are forgotten,
which I hate to forget
Will always find…

I am cheap,
but the scars and the struggles those who mark me
will never be cloned.

I still speak to her.

When she was happy and cheerful.
When I saw her Egyptian people,
when they were together with one heart,
one dream.
When they all cared for each other.
When it was a beautiful feeling.
When she loved her land,
but her people refused to keep her alive.

Letter

I am writing this letter with a smile
to think of you in my heart
diving into the details of someone's
existence.

This heart is beating like a song
with rhythm trying to escape from the chest
make his way alone without asking
just giving himself like if he is a wild animal
trying to eat her alive.

When I hug myself in pain
I try to relieve
love is everything by itself.

This is an unexplained error in my brain.
It is a transition but with a little of anger mixed with
sadness
to those who are alive and missing.

It is a sweet-sour candy taking my soul
to rest but my body to dirt
making me awake and others to shake.

After finishing my life,

how did I do in my existence?

The Nile River meets the Mediterranean Sea
one sweet and the other salty.
Between them is a barrier
trying to separate people from people
when you love someone, there is no limit.

We are all the same humans
same people
same world.

Whoever invented borders must be crazy!

Don't tell me to go because I will not.
It is not your decision if I am here or there.
You can't stop me, even if you try and mark the link.
I will step on it.
This is mine.
It will always be.
You can keep shouting,
but I will keep fighting.

Loving your life does not have a price.
Keep on loving each second in your life,
borders will not divide us.

Afterword

Congratulations to all those who participated in (insert name of project/book) for creating such moving and inspiring writing, and for sharing their stories with us throughout the project.

Writing on the Wall, the Liverpool City Region's Arts Organisation of the Year, celebrates writing in all its forms through our two annual festivals and year-round projects, working with a broad and inclusive definition of writing embracing literature, creative writing, journalism, nonfiction, poetry, song writing and storytelling.

We work with diverse communities across the Liverpool City Region to promote and celebrate individual and collective creativity, publishing high-quality work and supporting health, wellbeing, and personal development.

If you have a story to tell, or would like to take part in, or work with WoW to develop a writing project, please get in touch – we'd love to hear from you.

Madeline Heneghan and Mike Morris
Co-Directors

info@writingonthewall.org.uk
www.writingonthewall.org.uk
0151 703 0020
@wowfest